ENGINEERING MARVELS

SKYSCRAPERS

Marne Ventura

LIGHTBOX
openlightbox.com

LIGHTBOX

Go to
www.openlightbox.com
and enter this book's
unique code.

ACCESS CODE

LBH49939

Lightbox is an all-inclusive digital solution for the teaching and learning of curriculum topics in an original, groundbreaking way. Lightbox is based on National Curriculum Standards.

STANDARD FEATURES OF LIGHTBOX

AUDIO High-quality narration using text-to-speech system

ACTIVITIES Printable PDFs that can be emailed and graded

SLIDESHOWS Pictorial overviews of key concepts

VIDEOS Embedded high-definition video clips

WEBLINKS Curated links to external, child-safe resources

TRANSPARENCIES Step-by-step layering of maps, diagrams, charts, and timelines

INTERACTIVE MAPS Interactive maps and aerial satellite imagery

QUIZZES Ten multiple choice questions that are automatically graded and emailed for teacher assessment

KEY WORDS Matching key concepts to their definitions

Contents

Chapter 1

Reaching For The Sky

The elevator door slid open. Amelia and her friends were 1,354 feet (413 meters) in the air. The students walked to the Skydeck. They stood at the top of the Willis Tower in Chicago, Illinois. From the glass structure, Amelia could see parts of four states. People on the sidewalk seemed as tiny as ants.

The Skydeck is on the 103rd floor of the Willis Tower in Chicago.

Builders have been reaching for the sky for ages. Pyramids in ancient Egypt were made of heavy stone. In the Middle Ages, builders used stone to construct churches and towers. These buildings had few windows, so they were cold and dark. And the structures couldn't be built too high. The weight of the stone would cause them to collapse.

Things started to change during the 1700s and 1800s. This period was known as the Industrial Revolution. It was a time when many new machines were being invented. Millions of people were moving away from the country to work in cities.

However, this created challenges for engineers. They had to figure out how to fit more homes and offices in the crowded cities. And then they had to make their buildings safe, comfortable, and fireproof.

New York City's Empire State Building was the world's tallest building from 1931 to 1972.

The Great **Pyramid of Giza** was the **tallest** structure in the world for more than **3,800 years.**

The **Leaning Tower of Pisa** weighs **16,000 Tons** (14,500 metric tons). It began to lean during construction, and has a slight banana shape due to the builders' efforts to correct it.

By 1800, **1 in 10** people in all of **Great Britain** lived in the city of **London.**

The Flatiron building in New York City narrows to just 6 feet (2 m) wide at Fifth Avenue.

Inventions such as **steel**, **concrete**, and elevators helped the engineers meet these challenges.

The word *skyscraper* was first used in the 1880s. That was when the Home Insurance Building was built in Chicago. At 10 stories high, it was the world's first skyscraper.

New building materials and designs soon led to taller buildings. The Empire State Building in New York City was completed in 1931. It had more than 100 stories. Today's skyscrapers have many stories for offices or living space. People recognize many cities by their **skylines**.

Experts predict that approximately 70 percent of the world's people will live in cities by 2050. Skyscrapers are one solution to fitting more people on less land. They keep cities from spreading outward. And they give each city its own look. Today, engineers are finding new ways to create amazing buildings that reach for the sky.

Chapter 2

Skyscraper Design

Skyscrapers must be safe, comfortable places for people to live and work. Engineers take many steps to ensure this. A skyscraper has to resist **forces** called **loads**.

Skyscrapers are designed with light and flexible materials. This makes them more resilient to earthquakes.

The dead load is the weight of the building materials. The live load is the weight of the people and things, such as furniture, inside the skyscraper.

Engineers also consider natural elements. These include wind, fire, and earthquakes. For example, wind blowing against a skyscraper is a strong load.

This causes the tower to flex and bend, similar to a tall blade of grass. Earth's gravity is another load. And earthquakes can cause unpredictable loads. A skyscraper needs to be stable and remain standing despite the forces that push against it.

A **foundation** supports a building. Taller buildings have heavier loads, so they need strong, deep foundations. Builders dig down through the upper layers of the soil.

The **Comcast Center** in Philadelphia has a **300,000**-gallon (1.1 million-liter) damper. This helps keep the building from **swaying**.

The concrete footings of **One World Trade Center**'s foundation reach more than **200 Feet** (61 m) below street level.

The Burj Khalifa can sway up to **6 feet** (2 m) at the very top.

Finally, they get to the stable **bedrock** layer. Then they pour concrete over steel bars. This makes the building's foundation. The foundation supports the building and adds stability.

Next, builders construct the frame of the skyscraper on top of the foundation. The frames of early skyscrapers were simple steel boxes with smaller boxes inside. Steel beams supported the weight of the building.

It took 22 million man-hours to build the Burj Khalifa in Dubai, UAE.

Later, designers used a system of frames or walls in the shape of a vertical tube. This allowed engineers to give the skyscrapers more floor space. They didn't need horizontal frames anymore. That meant the buildings were lighter and could be higher.

The vertical tube design also created an inner core. Designers installed elevators here. The lighter core formed a strong backbone. It helped the building resist wind and other forces. It also took the load off of the exterior walls. Since the outer walls were not load-bearing, designers could use materials such as glass on the building's exterior. This let in lots of light. It also looked nice.

Skyscrapers must also be designed for people to use them. People need to be able to move easily up and down the building. The temperature and humidity needs to be comfortable. The building needs electricity. It also needs plumbing.

At 2,073 feet (632 m) tall, Shanghai Tower is the tallest skyscraper in China.

The planners must consider the design, too. They want people to be amazed and inspired when they look up at their buildings. An engineer must consider all of these factors when planning a skyscraper.

The Lloyd's Building in London, England, is sometimes called the "Inside-Out Building" for its unique design.

Engineering Design Process

Engineers use various tools and do many tests in their planning. Once a skyscraper is built, they expect the design to be safe and sturdy.

ASK Where will the skyscraper be built? What will it be used for? How many people will it need to fit? What materials are available?

IMAGINE Brainstorm possible skyscraper designs. Think of an idea that is unique but safe.

PLAN Draw a diagram of the skyscraper. Make a list of the materials needed. Write down the steps that will need to be taken to build it.

CREATE Follow the plan to build the skyscraper.

IMPROVE What worked with the skyscraper? What could be improved? How could the design change to make the skyscraper taller?

Chapter 3

Building a Skyscraper

Terrorists destroyed the World Trade Center towers in New York City on September 11, 2001. A new tower, One World Trade Center, was to be a memorial to the people who died there. But the new tower also needed to be safe and strong. Planners wanted it to use new technology and be environmentally friendly, too.

The One World Trade Center took 11 years to build.

The building site was in the middle of crowded New York City. Train tracks and subway tracks were already in place. So, engineers had to find a way to lay a strong foundation over these tracks. They designed steel bridges to support the concrete **anchor**. They also used a concrete core and steel frame for the skyscraper. In addition, they designed a shape that would decrease the building's wind load.

One World Trade Center has 70 elevators and a special stairway for fire and safety workers. Parts of the building are made with recycled materials. The glass sides let in sunlight so that less electricity is needed. Rainwater is used to cool the tower and to water plants.

The height of One World Trade Center is 1,776 feet (541 m). This number was a **tribute** to the year the United States became a nation. When the building opened in May 2015, it was the tallest skyscraper in the United States. Only three skyscrapers in the world were taller.

The One World Trade Center has an identical footprint to the original Twin Towers.

Chapter 4

Burj Khalifa is more than 160 stories tall.

Burj Khalifa

In January 2010, builders completed work on Burj Khalifa, a skyscraper in Dubai, United Arab Emirates. At 2,717 feet (828 m), it was by far the tallest building in the world. And because of its modern design, Burj Khalifa is half the weight of the Empire State Building. But it is twice as high.

The **architects** and engineers made the building with a Y-shaped floor plan. This shape is stable. It limits the wind pressure against the building. It also creates good space for living. In addition, this gives people a better view of the Arabian Gulf. Burj Khalifa contains 900 homes, 37 floors of office space, 57 elevators, 8 escalators, and a hotel. It also has 5 swimming pools.

Mapping Skyscrapers

Although the United States does not have the tallest skyscrapers in the world, it certainly has some of the best-known. The map shows where some of these engineering marvels are found. What is the tallest skyscraper near where you live?

Willis Tower

Chicago, Illinois

Height: 1,451 feet (442 m)

Construction of Sears Tower was completed in 1973. In 2009, it was officially renamed Willis Tower.

One World Trade Center

New York City, New York

Height: 1,776 feet (541 m)

One World Trade Center, also known as the Freedom Tower, was completed in 2013. It took the place of the World Trade Center buildings destroyed on 9/11. Currently, it is the tallest building in the Western Hemisphere.

Empire State Building

New York City, New York

Height: 1,250 feet (381 m)

The Empire State Building opened in 1931 and was the world's tallest building for more than 40 years.

Timeline

Today, skyscrapers mark the skylines of many cities across the United States. They make space for people to live and work in densely populated areas. Discover more about the history of skyscrapers in the United States.

1885

The Home Insurance Building is constructed in Chicago, Illinois. It is the first steel-frame skyscraper in the United States.

1901

The Temple Bar Building becomes New York's first skyscraper constructed outside of Manhattan.

1931

The Waldorf-Astoria Hotel is completed in New York, occupying an entire city block. At the time, it was the world's largest hotel.

1974

The Aon Center in Chicago is built. At the time, it was the world's tallest marble-clad building. It was covered in more than 43,000 slabs of Italian marble.

2014

The tallest all-residential skyscraper in the world, 432 Park Ave., is completed in New York City.

2017

The first U.S. skyscraper made primarily from wood is expected to be completed. This 12-story building will be located in Portland, Oregon.

Skyscraper Challenge

Now it's your turn to be an engineer. Build the tallest skyscraper you can. Try to use as few materials as possible to keep the structure light.

Materials

For this challenge you'll need craft sticks, clothespins, binder clips, and a table to work on.

Procedure

1. Plan a shape for your skyscraper. Do you want the base to be a square or a triangle? What about a rectangle?

2. Begin connecting the wooden craft sticks using the clothespins and binder clips.

3. Continue adding more sticks to go higher and higher. But be sure to test the structure to make sure it can stand on its own.

Considerations

Create wind against the side of your skyscraper by blowing or fanning. Does it remain standing?

Create an earthquake. Place your skyscraper on a piece of cardboard, and slide the cardboard back and forth. Does your skyscraper remain sturdy?

Improve It!

Can you change the foundation shape to make your skyscraper taller?

Experiment with different widths, heights, and shapes. How can you use the same materials to make a stronger shape?

Are there any materials you can remove without affecting the strength of your skyscraper?

Quiz

1 On what floor is the Skydeck located in Willis Tower?

2 What is the period during the 1700s and 1800s called?

3 How many stories high was the Home Insurance Building?

4 What is the weight of the people and things inside a skyscraper called?

5 What was the original name of Willis Tower?

6 How much does the Leaning Tower of Pisa weigh?

7 How many elevators does One World Trade Center have?

8 Burj Khalifa's floor plan is shaped like what letter of the alphabet?

9 What is the height of One World Trade Center a tribute to?

10 What structure was the tallest in the world for more than 3,800 years?

Answers

1. The 103rd floor **2.** The Industrial Revolution **3.** 10 **4.** Live load **5.** Sears Tower **6.** 16,000 tons (14,500 metric tons) **7.** 70 **8.** Y **9.** The year the United States became a nation **10.** The Great Pyramid of Giza

Key Words

anchor: A strong support that holds something in place

architects: People who design buildings

bedrock: The layer of solid rock under soil

concrete: A strong, stone-like material made from gravel, sand, cement, and water

forces: Pushes or pulls that happen when one object interacts with another object

foundation: The supporting base of a structure

loads: Masses or weights supported by something

skylines: The outlines of cities' tallest buildings against the background of the sky

steel: A strong metal made with iron, carbon, and other materials

terrorists: People who use violence to achieve a political goal

tribute: an act, gift, or statement given to express gratitude or esteem

Index

LIGHTBOX

SUPPLEMENTARY RESOURCES

Click on the plus icon ⊕ found in the bottom left corner of each spread to open additional teacher resources.

- Download and print the book's quizzes and activities
- Access curriculum correlations
- Explore additional web applications that enhance the Lightbox experience

LIGHTBOX DIGITAL TITLES
Packed full of integrated media

VIDEOS

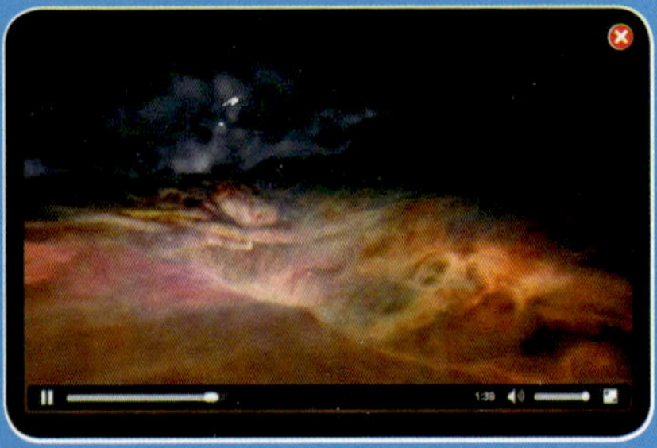

INTERACTIVE MAPS

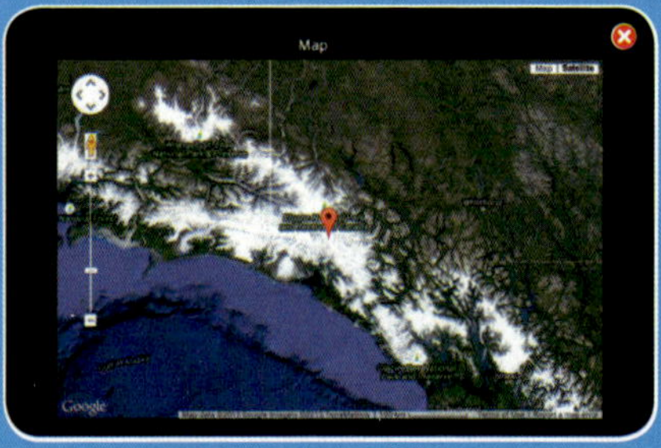

WEBLINKS

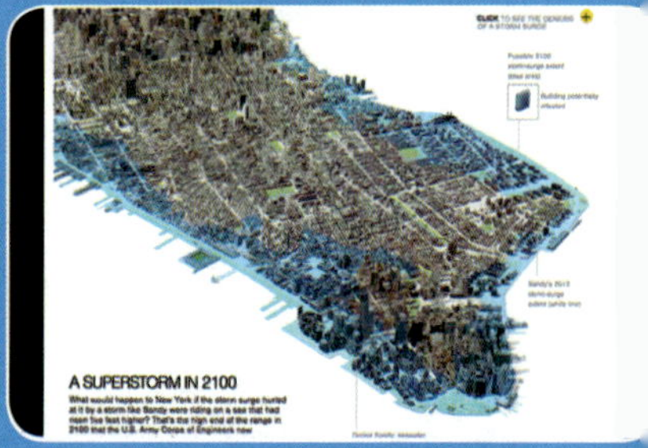

SLIDESHOWS

QUIZZES

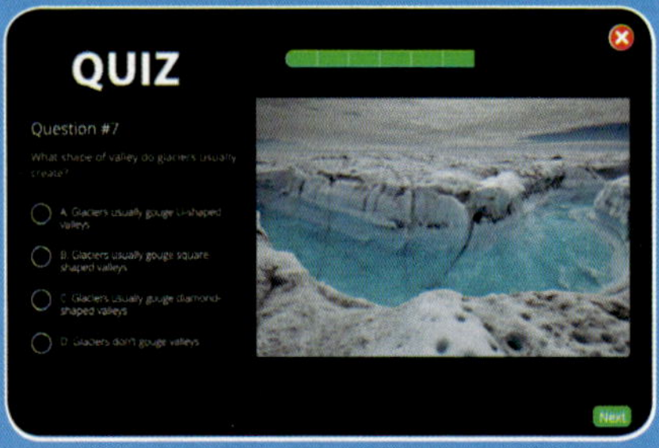

OPTIMIZED FOR

- ✓ TABLETS
- ✓ WHITEBOARDS
- ✓ COMPUTERS
- ✓ AND MUCH MORE!

Published by Smartbook Media Inc.
350 5th Avenue, 59th Floor New York, NY 10118
Website: www.openlightbox.com

012018
151217

Library of Congress Control Number: 2017961994

ISBN 978-1-5105-3736-1 (hardcover)
ISBN 978-1-5105-3737-8 (multi-user eBook)

Printed in the Brainerd, Minnesota, United States
1 2 3 4 5 6 7 8 9 0 22 21 20 19 18

First published by North Star Editions in 2018.

Project Coordinator: Jared Siemens
Designer: Ana María Vidal

Every reasonable effort has been made to trace ownership and to obtain permission to reprint copyright material. The publisher would be pleased to have any errors or omissions brought to its attention so that they may be corrected in subsequent printings.

The publisher acknowledges Alamy, Dreamstime, Getty Images, iStock, and Shutterstock as the primary image suppliers for this title.